IMAGES
of Rail

LONG ISLAND
RAIL ROAD
MONTAUK BRANCH

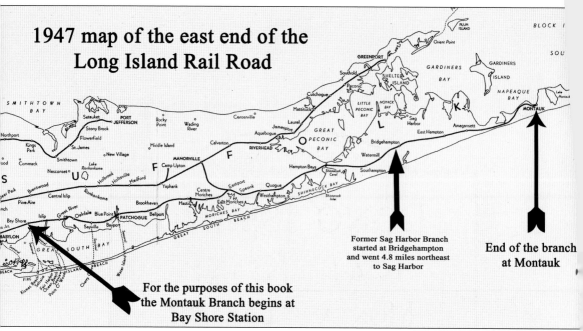

1947 map of the east end of the Long Island Rail Road

Former Sag Harbor Branch started at Bridgehampton and went 4.8 miles northeast to Sag Harbor

End of the branch at Montauk

For the purposes of this book the Montauk Branch begins at **Bay Shore Station**

This 1947 map shows the 24 Montauk Branch stations that existed east of Babylon. From Bay Shore to the terminal at Montauk, there were 32 stations at one time or another. Today, there are 16 stations on this 75-mile stretch of track, which is non-electrified, diesel-locomotive-only territory. (Author's collection.)

ON THE COVER: Passengers are ready to board the train in this 1907 photograph featuring Sayville Station. The building looks basically the same today, but gone are the railroad cars with windows that opened, horse carriages, and semaphore signal blades. The parking lots were unpaved, as indicated by the visible carriage-wheel tracks. (Author's collection.)

IMAGES
of Rail

LONG ISLAND
RAIL ROAD
MONTAUK BRANCH

David D. Morrison
Foreword by Steve Barry

ARCADIA
PUBLISHING

Published by Arcadia Publishing
Charleston, South Carolina

Printed in the United States of America

Library of Congress Control Number: 2021936336

For all general information, please contact Arcadia Publishing:
Telephone 843-853-2070
Fax 843-853-0044
E-mail sales@arcadiapublishing.com
For customer service and orders:
Toll-Free 1-888-313-2665

Visit us on the Internet at www.arcadiapublishing.com

This book is dedicated to Bernardino F. Genchi, a 1964 Islip High School graduate who gave his life in the service of his country in Viet Nam on July 22, 1969. (See pages 20–21.)

CONTENTS

FOREWORD

The Sunrise Trail is one of those legendary names that gets attached to railroads and becomes synonymous with the line. In this case, the Sunrise Trail refers to the Long Island Rail Road (LIRR) and, more specifically, its service to the eastern end of the island at Montauk. While people living east of New York City will most often think of the LIRR as the busiest commuter system in the United States, it is the Montauk Branch that comes to mind when the rest of the country considers the railroad. Trains with names like the Sunrise Special and the Cannonball—with parlor cars filled with New York's rich and famous heading for a weekend away from the city—are the LIRR's claim to fame to many people.

There is no better guide to the LIRR than Dave Morrison. I first encountered Dave in my role as editor of *Railfan & Railroad* magazine when he pitched me a story about the eagles that adorned Grand Central Station (the predecessor to Grand Central Terminal). While we generally run stories about locomotives and rail lines in the magazine, the story was just quirky enough—and Dave's research was thorough and engaging enough—that I decided our readers might enjoy it even though it was a bit out of our usual coverage. And I was right; everyone found the story interesting. This led me to explore more of Dave's research into the overlooked, especially when he turned his attention to tracking down the eagles of Pennsylvania Station (which is, not coincidentally, the western terminus of the LIRR).

Over the years, I have found Dave to be the go-to person for LIRR history. His previous Arcadia Publishing books on the railroad, taken as a whole, provide one of the finest collections of historic photographs of the railroad. This book brings the most recognized segment of the LIRR to the forefront.

Before you dig deeper into this book, join me in pouring a glass of your favorite adult beverage, lighting up a cigar, settling in, and imagining you are on a parlor car heading for Montauk. With Dave Morrison as our guide, this will be a trip full of memories on the Sunrise Trail.

Steve Barry
Editor, *Railfan & Railroad* magazine

ACKNOWLEDGMENTS

With this being my ninth book in Arcadia Publishing's Images of Rail series, I owe a lot of credit to David Keller for helping me with my books through the years. He has a treasure trove of historical Long Island Rail Road documents and photographs in his archives, which he has readily shared with me. He has also performed meticulous editing of text.

A special word of thanks to Steve Barry, editor of *Railfan & Railroad* magazine, for writing such a persuasive foreword, which I consider to be quite an honor to me.

Much appreciation goes to friends who helped me with information and images that made this book worthy of publication in the Images of Rail series: Win A. Boerckel, Michael Boland, Don Fisher, Don Konrad, Steve Lynch, Carol Mills-Nichol, Robert Myers, Brad Phillips, Larry Shea, and Steve Quigley.

The book includes praiseworthy work by the following artists: Elizabeth Duerschmidt (Westhampton Station painting), Howard Fogg (Montauk painting commissioned by John Scala), Edward Lange (Patchogue painting), and Tom Pepper (Oakdale Station drawing). A photograph of the bust of LIRR president Austin Corbin was provided courtesy of the Putnam Museum and Science Center of Davenport, Iowa.

Appreciation goes to those who contributed photographs of the late warrant officer Bernadino F. Genchi: Rosalie Goebel (his cousin) and Dina Soriano (his daughter).

The Patchogue-Medford Library was a great source for photographs.

The Sag Harbor freight house—now the home of the Sag Harbor Garden Center—offers a great example of the reuse of a historic building. Sag Harbor Garden Center proprietors Diane and Phil Bucking provided fascinating information and photographs.

Highly reliant sources of information include the seven-volume history of the LIRR by Vincent F. Seyfried, as well as the numerous books of Ron Ziel. By far, the best website for LIRR historical information is www.trainsarefun.com.

Caitrin Cunningham and Jim Kempert of Arcadia Publishing provided much input and guidance.

Finally, appreciation goes to my wife, Diane, who had the patience to see me complete another book in the Images of Rail series.

Images are from the author's collection unless otherwise credited.

INTRODUCTION

For the purposes of this book, the Montauk Branch will encompass the Long Island Rail Road stations on the south shore of Long Island from Bay Shore to Montauk. This 75-mile stretch of railroad is non-electrified (meaning there is no third rail) diesel locomotive territory. The electrified third rail terminates at Babylon, which is the first station west of Bay Shore. The Montauk Branch is double-track to east of Sayville, where it goes into single-track for the remainder of the way to the eastern terminal at Montauk. The branch was developed by the South Side Rail Road (SSRR), which laid tracks as far as Patchogue in 1869. The SSRR was absorbed by the LIRR in 1876.

There is a seven-track layup yard at Speonk with a wye for turning trains. There is a six-track layup yard at Montauk, also with a wye to allow trains to be turned. Along the branch, there are numerous passing sidings to allow eastbound and westbound trains to safely pass each other. The entire branch to Montauk is now governed by an automatic block signal system controlled from Babylon Tower, since PD Tower in Patchogue was removed from service and demolished in 2006.

It could be said that this book completes the Long Island Rail Road east end trilogy in the Images of Rail series of Arcadia Publishing books. On the north shore, the LIRR ends at Port Jefferson, which is covered in *Long Island Rail Road: Port Jefferson Branch*. On the north fork, the LIRR ends at Greenport, which is covered in *Long Island Rail Road: Main Line East*. On the south fork, the LIRR ends at Montauk, which is covered herein.

This book also completes the coverage of LIRR non-electrified territory, which includes the stations east of Huntington, the stations east of Ronkonkoma, the stations on the Oyster Bay Branch east of East Williston, and—as featured in this book—the stations east of Babylon.

The railroad at Montauk is a popular location for photographing trains with the picturesque Montauk Manor Hotel overlooking the terminal facilities from the bluff in the background. On Thursday and Friday evenings, trains arriving at Montauk were stored over the weekend for the Sunday night and Monday morning return runs to New York City. On the Montauk Branch, the LIRR's famous all-parlor-car train, Cannonball, used to bring passengers from New York City to the south shore resort towns in the Hamptons.

In the past, east end trains would have baggage cars and railway post office cars at the head, and on parlor car trains, open-end observation cars at the rear. The LIRR made arrangements to, at various times, use baggage cars for vacationers to store their bicycles and for those on "Fishermen's Specials" to store their fishing gear and coolers.

Between Hampton Bays and Shinnecock Hills, the railroad crosses over a steel-girder bridge going across the majestic Shinnecock Canal. There were two earlier bridges since the canal was dug in 1892. In 1931, a new bridge was erected that was 212 feet long and weighed 800 tons, allowing the heaviest locomotives to safely traverse.

This book is divided into eight chapters:

Chapter 1: Bay Shore to Club House. The beautiful Dutch Colonial building erected in 1912 is still the active passenger station at Bay Shore. There is quite a story behind the weather vane on the 1963 Islip Station building. Great River has a one-of-a-kind passenger shelter shed.

Chapter 2: Oakdale to Blue Point. The 1890 Oakdale Station is known as the "wedding station." The 1905 station building at Sayville still serves LIRR customers, although the stations at Bayport and Blue Point have long been dropped from the timetable.

Chapter 3: Patchogue. Once the eastern terminal of the South Side Rail Road, Patchogue is best known for the 1912 wooden signal tower that was 100 yards east of the station building and escaped a planned demolition in 1963. Sadly, it was demolished in 2006.

Chapter 4: Hagerman to Eastport. At one time, there were seven stations between these two locations; today, only two exist—Bellport and Mastic Shirley. The LIRR ran trains from Manorville (on the Greenport main line) to Eastport until 1949.

Chapter 5: Speonk and Westhampton. The 1901 Speonk Station building still exists, although it is not currently in use. The high-level platforms are west of the former station location. The 1905 Westhampton Station building was nearly lost to fire twice but survives today in all of its beauty.

Chapter 6: Quogue to Watermill. There were once seven stations between these two locations; today, only two exist—Hampton Bays and Southampton. A station west of Southampton once served students at the Southampton College, as well as attendees at four US Open championship golf tournaments.

Chapter 7: Bridgehampton to Amagansett. Seven stations are covered in this chapter. Because the Sag Harbor line branched off at Bridgehampton, the Noyack Road and Sag Harbor stations are included. Also included is one station that was east of Amagansett—Napeague Beach. The two flag stops between Amagansett and Napeague Beach, Promised Land and Bartlett, are only mentioned here in this introduction.

Chapter 8: Montauk. This is the end of the line for the branch. It is the easternmost station on the LIRR—and the easternmost railroad station in New York State. The destination for those getting off the train at this final stop is often the famous Montauk lighthouse, which is a short drive from the station through Hither Hills State Park. The landmark lighthouse has been featured as a promotional item on LIRR brochures, timetables, and other literature throughout the years. The lighthouse symbolizes the end of the Sunrise Trail, which is a phrase once used to refer to the railroad that ends at the eastern end of Long Island.

The emphasis in this book is on the railroad stations of the Montauk Branch. When a person takes a trip on the railroad, the first and last thing that they will see is a station. The stations are what give an impression of a location. In this author's opinion, it could be said that trains were created to give purpose to the stations.

For more information about LIRR history, recommended reading includes various books in Arcadia Publishing's Images of Rail series. Eight such books were written by this author, and two were written by David Keller and Steven Lynch. Other reading includes the books of Michael Boland, Stan Fischler, John Scala, Vincent Seyfried, Robert Sturm, and Ron Ziel. By far, the best website for LIRR history is trainsarefun.com, which is run by Steven Lynch and David Keller with support from the Long Island Sunrise Trail Chapter of the National Railway Historical Society.

40.7	Bayshore........
43.1	Islip.............
45.2	Great River ......
47.4	Oakdale.........
49.8	Sayville..........
51 5	Bayport..........
52.5	Blue Point.......
53.9	Patchogue.......
57.7	Bellport..........
59.6	Brookhaven......
63.7	Mastic...........
66.3	Centre Moriches..
67.7	East Moriches....
......	Manorville.......
......	Eastport.........
69.9	Eastport..........
71.4	Speonk..........
74.3	Westhampton.....
77.0	Quogue..........
82.0	Good Ground.....
83.6	Suffolk Downs....
85.4	Shinnecock Hills
86.6	Golf Grounds.....
89.2	Southampton.....
91.9	Watermill........
94.5	Bridgehampton...
97.0	Wainscott........
100.9	Easthampton.....
104.3	Amagansett......
109.8	Napeague Beach..
115 7.	Montauk.........

This is a list of stations that appeared on LIRR employee timetable No. 50, effective November 5, 1908. The left column shows the miles from Long Island City; Penn Station service did not begin until 1910. The distance from Bay Shore to Montauk was 75 miles. Manorville is a station on the main line, but it appears on the list because a track from that station connected with the Montauk Branch at Eastport. Bridgehampton is where a short branch extended to Sag Harbor. Club House (east of Great River) and Hagerman (east of Patchogue) are not listed.

One

BAY SHORE TO CLUB HOUSE

The South Side Rail Road started service to Babylon on October 28, 1867. Within months, track-laying had proceeded farther east, and on May 20, 1868, trains began running to the village of Penataquit. In July 1868, the village changed its name to Bay Shore. This photograph of the first Bay Shore Station building was taken by George Brainerd in September 1879. In 1882, this wood-frame building was destroyed by fire.

After the original Bay Shore Station building burned down in 1882, a wood-frame structure was erected with canopies on each side to shelter waiting passengers. The early-1900s postcard above shows an impressive overview of the 1882 station looking northeast. The carriages at the station were the taxicabs of that time. The 1905 photograph below looks west and shows a train at the platform with crew members standing on the wooden structure. The jigsaw trim below the canopy is quite decorative, as is the station destination sign featuring "Bayshore" spelled as one word. Up until 1938, LIRR timetables show Bayshore as one word, but in 1939, the station's name was spelled "Bay Shore." To add to the confusion, look at the following image.

The R. R Station,
Bay Shore, L. I.

This postcard looks west and has a 1910 postmark on the reverse. It shows the "Bayshore" sign on the station building, yet the card identifies it as "Bay Shore." Evidently, both spellings of the village's name were used throughout the early 1900s. Horse carriages are at the east end of the station, while an early automobile—with the steering wheel on the right side—is in the foreground. The passenger coach's windows are open, indicating that the picture was taken during warm weather.

RAILROAD STATION.   BAY SHORE, LONG ISLAND, N. Y.

The 1882 wood-frame Bay Shore Station building on the south side of the tracks was demolished in early 1912, and on July 17, 1912, a new two-story brick building opened on the north side. There was a brick waiting room building on the south side with a pedestrian underpass. This undated postcard looks northeast and shows vintage automobiles parked at the station and passengers boarding an eastbound train with some of its windows open.

The 1912 Bay Shore Station building, which still exists today, was a Dutch Colonial–style, brick-and-wood-frame structure with a gambrel roof and substantial canopies on each side. This valuation photograph, looking northwest, was taken on October 23, 1917. Other stations with this design may be seen at Huntington, Bayside, Manhasset, Mineola, Northport, and Riverhead. Sadly, two similar buildings were demolished at Hampton Bays and Amagansett, as discussed in chapters six and seven.

LIRR Claims Department photographer Fred J. Weber took this picture looking north toward the First Street grade crossing in Bay Shore on September 29, 1933. The grade crossing watchman is standing in the middle of the street. The watchman's shanty is at right, across the tracks, and it is evident that there were no crossing gates in place at this time.

This May 6, 1949, photograph by Fred J. Weber looks east and shows the Bay Shore Station building as well as the eastbound waiting room on the opposite side of the tracks. The Park Avenue grade crossing is in the foreground. In 1984, high-level platforms were installed at the station, and this grade crossing was permanently closed. In 2009, a pedestrian overpass was constructed in this area, and the underpass between the station and the waiting room was closed and permanently sealed.

The LIRR was evidently so impressed by the beauty of the Bay Shore Station building that it placed a photograph of it on the cover of the August 1950 issue of the *Long Island Railroader* employee magazine. The wooden fence between the tracks prevented pedestrians from crossing at undesignated spots. High-level platforms now prevent a view such as this at the station.

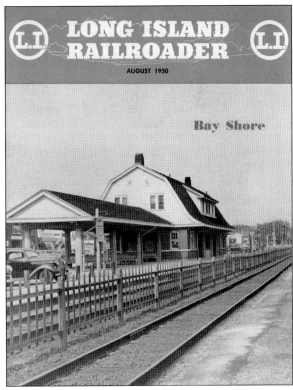

LONG ISLAND RAILROADER

L.I.   L.I.

AUGUST 1950

Bay Shore

These images look southwest toward the eastbound waiting room building. In the photograph at left, which was taken by James V. Osborne in the 1920s, is a tower that was added to the structure's roof sometime after 1917. That tower, which is shrouded in mystery, was removed by 1930. The Fred J. Weber photograph below was taken on May 6, 1949, and shows the structure at a similar angle with no tower. The milepost marker, designated with a large "40," is at the east end of the building, and the Park Avenue grade crossing is in the distance at right.

The first depot in Islip, which opened on May 20, 1869, had wide canopies surrounding the building, and the entire structure was mounted on posts. The South Side Rail Road often painted a station's name in large lettering on the exterior wall of the building. In this photograph, birdhouses are visible at the trackside edges of the canopy roof. However, smoke from locomotives probably prevented birds from finding a nesting place in these decorative fixtures.

In this c. 1879 view of the original Islip depot, the express house is at the far end of the station platform. Note the absence of the birdhouses and the painted station name. The route through this station was single track without any passing siding. Movable wooden benches are visible on the platform. This building was demolished in 1881, when a new building was erected.

In 1881, the original Islip Station building was replaced by a larger wood-frame building with a surrounding canopy. The structure was on a raised platform, and decorative features were added to enhance its appearance. Sawtooth trim was placed along the bottom edge of the canopy, and an ornate wooden crest was at the top of the roof's ridgeline. This 1911 photograph shows a westbound train at the station.

This 1919 postcard featuring the Islip Station is loaded with historic details. It offers a great view of the sawtooth canopy trim as well as a water pump in the left foreground and the express house in the distance at left. The men on the roof are evidently removing the roof crest. A concrete base had been poured around the building, but the surrounding plaza was still dirt.

LIRR Claims Department photographer Fred J. Weber was authorized to take pictures at railroad facilities during World War II. He captured this peaceful scene looking west at Islip Station on June 6, 1944, a date later recognized worldwide as "D-Day." A pathway is shown going across the tracks from the station building to the shelter shed. At left, in the far distance at trackside, is the coal pockets structure of the Islip Coal and Feed Company.

This 1915 photograph shows the coal pockets structure east of Commack Road. Constructed in 1910 for the Islip Coal and Feed Company, this allowed railroad hopper cars to dump coal into a pit below the track. The slanted structure contained the bucket-conveyor that carried coal from the pit to the storage bins in the superstructure. Highway trucks were then filled at street level before transporting the coal to businesses and residences.

The Islip Coal and Feed Co.

DEALERS IN

Coal, Wood, Feed Hay Grain and Straw

At Lowest Market Prices

"You'll Like Our Weigh"

Yard and Office Near Depot   Main Office, MAIN STREET

Telephone 1122

In 1963, the 1881 Islip Station building was demolished, and a new building designed by local architect Richard F. Boyd was erected. This Colonial-style building had an overhanging roof surrounding the structure, and there was a cupola in the center of the roof. The building was dedicated on Saturday, December 6, 1963. Islip High School student Bernardino F. Genchi highlighted the ceremony by placing a locomotive weather vane on top of the cupola. The lighting company provided a cherry-picker to lift Genchi so that he could affix the weather vane that he made as an industrial arts student. Shortly after graduating from high school in June 1964, Genchi enlisted in the US Army.

Bernardino F. Genchi was assigned to the 135th Aviation Company in Viet Nam. He was killed in Viet Nam on July 22, 1969, while the helicopter that he was piloting crashed. This banner is mounted in his honor at the corner of Main Street and Union Avenue in Islip. As well as being honored by his community, Genchi certainly has a place in the legacy of the LIRR

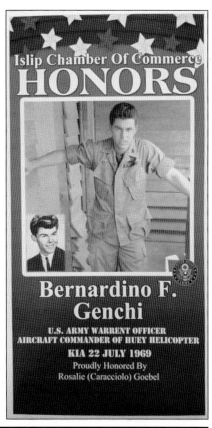

Islip Chamber Of Commerce

HONORS

Bernardino F. Genchi

U.S. ARMY WARRENT OFFICER
AIRCRAFT COMMANDER OF HUEY HELICOPTER

KIA 22 JULY 1969

Proudly Honored By
Rosalie (Caracciolo) Goebel

There are 58,318 names on the Vietnam Veterans Memorial in Washington, DC. One of the names is Bernardino Francis Genchi, at panel 20W, line 33. This image is from the Vietnam Veterans Memorial website. Genchi was laid to rest at the Long Island National Cemetery in Farmingdale, New York.

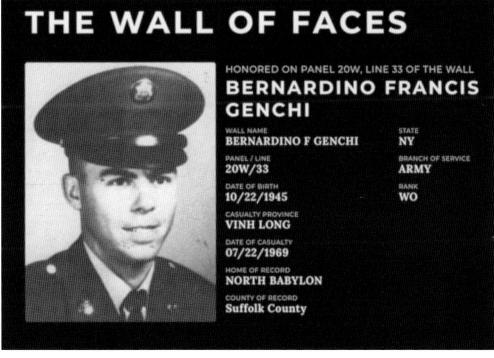

THE WALL OF FACES

HONORED ON PANEL 20W, LINE 33 OF THE WALL

BERNARDINO FRANCIS GENCHI

WALL NAME	STATE
BERNARDINO F GENCHI	NY

PANEL / LINE	BRANCH OF SERVICE
20W/33	ARMY

DATE OF BIRTH	RANK
10/22/1945	WO

CASUALTY PROVINCE
VINH LONG

DATE OF CASUALTY
07/22/1969

HOME OF RECORD
NORTH BABYLON

COUNTY OF RECORD
Suffolk County

In 1897, the LIRR opened a passenger station at Great River, erecting a building with a porte cochere on the street side. An express/baggage house was west of the building, and a shelter shed was across the tracks. This 1925 photograph taken by James V. Osborne shows an eastbound freight train being pulled by a steam locomotive. Note the kerosene lamps on the station platforms.

On March 23, 1945, the original Great River Station building was destroyed by fire. In this image, volunteer firemen are holding up the station sign, which they rescued from the fire. The shelter shed, which was on the north side of the tracks, is in the background. A small brick station building was erected after the fire, but was demolished in 1998, leaving only the shelter shed.

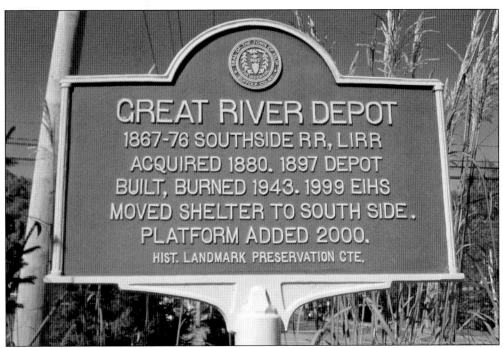

The shelter shed that survived the 1945 station fire was moved by the East Islip Historical Society to the south side of the tracks in 1999. Above is a photograph of the plaque placed at the station. The plaque incorrectly states that the station burned in 1943—the March 24, 1945, edition of *Newsday* reported that the fire occurred the previous day. The placement of the shelter shed, as shown in the October 11, 2016, photograph below, defies logic. Railroad shelter sheds are normally placed parallel to the tracks so that people can look out of the front of the shed in either direction to see if a train is approaching. This shed is oriented perpendicular to the tracks. For a person to see an eastbound train approaching, they would have to step outside the shed and look around it. At least the structure was nicely preserved.

In 1870, Club House Station was created as a flag stop to serve patrons visiting the nearby South Side Sportsmen's Club. A small box-type building was constructed between what are now the Great River and Oakdale Stations. In the style often utilized by the South Side Rail Road, large lettering was placed on the sides of the building, as shown in this 1878 photograph taken by George Brainerd. The building was demolished when the stop was removed from the timetable in 1885.

This February 16, 2020, photograph shows the beauty of the South Side Sportsmen's Club. Notable members of the club included Theodore Roosevelt, Andrew Carnegie, and William K. Vanderbilt. An 1886 building expansion was designed by Bradford Lee Gilbert, who also designed the LIRR's Bayport, Southampton, and Oyster Bay Stations. In 1973, the club closed, and the property was turned over to the State of New York and is now part of the Connetquot River State Park Preserve.

Two

OAKDALE TO BLUE POINT

In 1868, the first station building opened in Oakdale. Fortunately, it was one of the stations that was photographed in 1878 by George Brainard, as seen here. In characteristic South Side Rail Road style, the name of the station was painted in large letters on the sides of the building. An outhouse is visible at far right and a freight house is in the distance at left. The second floor probably served as living quarters for the station agent and their family.

The estate of William K. Vanderbilt was known as Idle Hour and was one mile west of the Oakdale train station. Legend has it that Vanderbilt wanted to have a distinctive station at Oakdale so that guests coming to his daughter's wedding could get off the train and into carriages for the ride to his estate. In 1890, he gave building plans and $20,000 to the LIRR, and the beautiful brick structure was erected; it is still in use as an active train station. The postcard image above looks northwest toward the station with a carriage house at far left. Two fireplace chimneys and a street-side porte cochere added to the unique look of the building. Below is a May 13, 1918, valuation photograph looking southwest toward the building. Two trackside dormers projected from the slate roof. This station became known as the "wedding station."

The above 1907 postcard view looks southeast and shows a westbound train being pulled by a smoke-billowing steam locomotive as it enters Oakdale Station. Also facing southeast is the below October 18, 2016, photograph showing that little has changed in the appearance of the building, although the chimney at the east end was removed. Fortunately, when high-level platforms were installed in the late 1990s, the eastbound platform did not extend far enough out to obstruct the view of the building. Although Dowling College ceased operation on August 31, 2016, the station destination signs had not yet been revised at the time this picture was taken.

The freight house at Oakdale is on the south side of the track a short distance west of the station building. In this 1941 photograph, an eastbound passenger train pulled by Pennsylvania Railroad steam locomotive No. 732 is approaching the freight house. This building still exists, but the lead track and platform have been demolished, and the building is only used for storage.

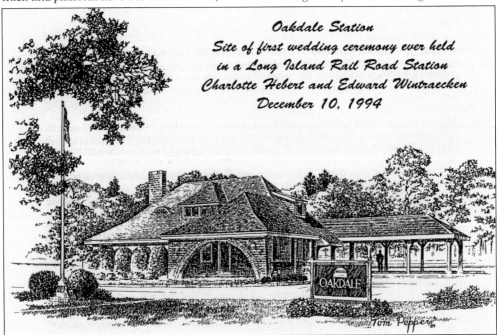

Oakdale Station
Site of first wedding ceremony ever held
in a Long Island Rail Road Station
Charlotte Hebert and Edward Wintraecken
December 10, 1994

On December 10, 1994, the first wedding ever held inside an LIRR railroad station took place at Oakdale when Charlotte Hebert and Edward Wintraecken got married in front of the waiting room fireplace. Long Island artist Tom Pepper granted permission for his Oakdale Station art print to be placed on the cover of the wedding program. Note that the chimney for the waiting room's fireplace had long been removed.

Charlotte Hebert contacted the author (the branch line manager at the time) a few months prior to her wedding date, saying that her fiancé was a railroad enthusiast and that she desired a railroad-themed wedding ceremony. The author then made the Oakdale waiting room available for the Saturday afternoon ceremony. Pictured here in front of the fireplace are Hebert and her husband, Edward Wintraecken, as well as other members of the wedding party. Ticket clerk Terry Henderson eagerly participated in the decoration of the room. After the ceremony, the couple posed in front of the Oakdale Station building. They gave true meaning to Oakdale being known as the "wedding station." Several weeks later, Hebert called to ask where she should send payment for the use of the station. After consulting with higher-ups, the author was pleased to inform her that she could "forget about it." This was a nice gesture from the LIRR.

In 1868, the South Side Rail Road opened a station at Sayville, erecting a wooden building with a large overhanging roof surrounding the structure, as shown in this c. 1902 photograph. A large group of people are standing outside the building on a cold winter day—note the snow on the ground and the bare trees in the left background. The uniformed man closest to the camera was probably the station agent.

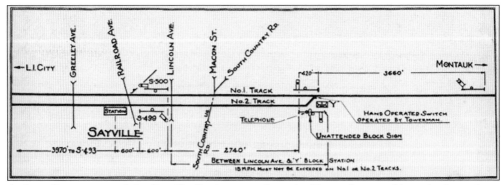

A short distance east of the Sayville Station was where double track merged into single track on the Montauk Branch. At this location, there was a hand-operated switch controlled by a block operator who was provided with a shelter known as the "Y" cabin.

This is the "Y" cabin east of Sayville Station where double track merged into single track for the remainder of the route to the terminal at Montauk. This James V. Osborne photograph faces east and shows the switch points controlled by the block operator. The cabin was moved to the south side of the tracks in 1930.

This 1910 postcard shows an eastbound train on the passing siding at Sayville. The people on the platform are probably waiting for the westbound train to New York City. A carriage is at the station, possibly ready to take people to the ferry docks. As was typical at the time, the ladies wear long dresses, and the men wear hats.

Passengers are ready to board the train in this 1907 photograph of Sayville Station. The building looks basically the same today, but gone are the railroad cars with windows that opened, horse carriages, and semaphore signal blades. The parking lot was dirt, as indicated by the visible carriage wheel tracks.

LIRR Claims Department photographer Fred J. Weber took this photograph at Sayville Station on April 12, 1946. A protective fence between the tracks prevented people from haphazardly crossing to the other side. There was a walkway opening in the fence with a gate mounted on a rolling mechanism that allowed the crossing to be closed whenever necessary for passenger safety.

The South Side Rail Road established a station stop at Bayport in March 1869, erecting a simple box-type wooden building, an express house a bit east, and an express platform to the west. This 1902 photograph looks east and shows the express loading platform at right and the station building farther down the track. The structures shown here were demolished in 1903 and replaced with a new station building.

This c. 1905 postcard view looks west and shows the Bayport Station building that opened on August 10, 1903. Designed by architect Bradford Lee Gilbert, the building was erected by LIRR workers—no outside contractors were hired. Constructed of concrete, this building lasted until it was razed in May 1964. The station stop was removed from the timetable on September 8, 1980.

This May 8, 1918, valuation photograph looks east and provides a trackside view of the Bayport Station building. The raised, eyebrow-style feature in the center of the trackside roofline gave the building a unique appearance. The track at left was a passing siding.

In addition to designing the Bayport Station building, architect Bradford Lee Gilbert designed two other LIRR station buildings: the one at Southampton (see pages 87 and 88) and Oyster Bay (see *Long Island Rail Road: Oyster Bay Branch*). As mentioned on page 24, Gilbert also designed a major part of the South Side Sportsmen's Club building. He is well known for his 1898 expansion of Grand Central Station in New York City.

The South Side Rail Road opened a station in Blue Point on February 1, 1870. A small, box-type building was erected with the characteristic SSRR large lettering painted on both ends of the building, as shown in this c. 1870 photograph taken by George Brainerd. The station stop was discontinued on June 1, 1882, due to low usage, and the building was demolished.

In 1900, the Blue Point station stop was reestablished, and a wood-frame building was erected with a wide roof overhang surrounding the structure. This early-1900s postcard view faces east, showing the single track with no passing siding at this station. This building was almost identical to the building at Speonk (see pages 68–71), although it sported a rear porte cochere. This building was torn down in 1951, and the station stop was discontinued on September 6, 1980.

This August 1, 1939, photograph by Fred J. Weber looks west and gives a great view of the small freight/express house east of the Blue Point station building. At left is a stub track that dead-ends at the building. A signal mast is at the far end of the platform.

In this Fred J. Weber photograph taken on April 4, 1944, the Blue Point station building is visible in the distance looking east from Blue Point Avenue. The stairway leads up to the station platform. According to railroad historian David Keller, the distant smokestack visible to the left of the station building belonged to the PELCO plant in Patchogue.

Three

PATCHOGUE STATION AND PD TOWER

Long Island artist Edward Lange created drawings and paintings of local scenes during the 1870s and 1880s. He painted five railroad scenes, including this 1876 painting of Patchogue River with the South Side Rail Road train shed in the center. His four other railroad scenes feature Woodbury (Cold Spring Harbor), Huntington, Greenlawn, and Northport, which can be seen in *Long Island Rail Road: Port Jefferson Branch.*

After crossing the Patchogue River, South Side Rail Road trains had access to a 220-foot-long train shed, as shown in this 1878 George Brainerd photograph looking east. The village of Patchogue is visible in the distance. Constructed in July/August 1869, this substantial train shed could fit four 40-foot wooden cars, plus a locomotive and tender, under its roof.

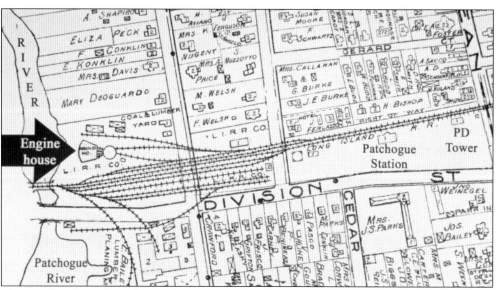

The South Side Rail Road started service at Patchogue on April 10, 1869, with trains running through Jamaica to the Brooklyn waterfront, where ferries would carry passengers across the East River to Manhattan. The SSRR never built past Patchogue due to the LIRR building the Sag Harbor Branch in 1869–1870. In 1876, the LIRR took over the SSRR. This c. 1920 map shows the LIRR facilities in Patchogue.

The emphasis of the c. 1920 photograph above is on the delivery of pianos from the Patchogue freight yard facility to the Ackerly Piano Store, as indicated on the delivery wagon. Fortunately, it also shows a rare view of the turntable and four-stall engine house. Installed in the early 1900s, this engine house was identical in design to the engine houses at Greenport and Oyster Bay. After the consolidation of all engine service facilities into the Morris Park Shop facility in 1928, the Patchogue engine house—and all others—were razed. The postcard below shows the Ackerly Piano Store on Ocean Avenue looking toward Main Street. (Above, courtesy of Patchogue-Medford Library.)

There are no known photographs or drawings of the original South Side Rail Road Patchogue depot. It appears that there are no newspaper articles pertaining to the April 10, 1869, start of train service at Patchogue. Evidently, there was no type of celebration held for that historic event. These two postcard views, both facing east, show the brick Victorian station building that opened at Patchogue in the summer of 1888. The canopies on both sides of the building were enhanced by elaborate Victorian decor. The peaked roof over the agent's bay added to the charm of the building. An identical building opened the same year at Sea Cliff on the Oyster Bay Branch. The 1888 Patchogue building was demolished on May 16, 1963. For anyone wanting to see what the 1888 Patchogue building looked like, a visit to Sea Cliff would suffice.

LIRR Claims Department photographer Fred J. Weber took these pictures facing east at Patchogue Station on May 19, 1943. This was during World War II, when photography at railroad facilities was against the law, but Weber had authority due to the nature of his job. In the above image, the agent's bay is clearly visible projecting out from the trackside of the building. The signal tower and position light signal are in the center distance. Below, it is apparent that Weber moved farther east to capture this view of the baggage house at right and the tower beyond.

In this photograph taken by Fred J. Weber on May 19, 1943 (the same day he took the two pictures on the previous page), the view faces west from the track in front of the baggage house. The steam locomotive water tank is visible beyond the station building, and advertising signs are next to the north siding track.

This 1912 postcard looks northwest toward the Patchogue Station building. Horse carriages are at the station, and wagon-wheel tracks are visible on the unpaved station grounds. This view captures the beauty of the Victorian station's canopy. The two chimneys on the building were for the potbelly stoves in the waiting room and ticket office.

This May 19, 1943, photograph by Fred J. Weber shows the steam locomotive water tank at left and the Railroad Avenue grade crossing. A freight house is in the distance at right, and beyond that is the high smokestack of the Patchogue Electric Lighting Company (PELCO) electricity plant.

Weber moved farther west from the location of the previous image to take this picture showing the West Avenue grade crossing with the steam locomotive servicing facility at distant right. The PELCO plant, with its smokestack in view, was located near the railroad to facilitate the delivery of coal by railroad hopper cars.

At the Patchogue locomotive servicing facility, two leased Pennsylvania Railroad 4-4-2 class E3sd steam locomotives are at the ash pit in this mid-1930s photograph taken by H. Reschke facing northwest. The West Avenue grade crossing is in the distance at right. (Courtesy of Patchogue-Medford Library.)

Railroad employees pose on May 16, 1913, on the front end of LIRR steam locomotive No. 139. Judging from their clothing, these seven men might have been an engine crew and maintenance employees. (Courtesy of Patchogue-Medford Library.)

At one time, there were 17 turntables on the LIRR. The one at Patchogue, which was designated No. 11, was a 70-foot, hand-operated turntable commonly known as an Armstrong turntable. Bill Slade took this picture of it facing southeast in 1955. A similar turntable is on display at the Greenport location of the Railroad Museum of Long Island.

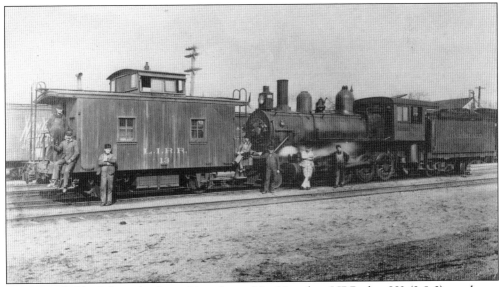

An LIRR "bobber" four-wheel wooden caboose No. 13 and an LIRR class H3 (2-8-0) are shown at the Patchogue yard in this 1915 photograph facing northeast. The employee seated at left was freight conductor Raymond Robinson Jr. of Eastport. The identities of the others are not known.

These two Fred J. Weber photographs were taken in 1943 and feature views facing east from the Railroad Avenue grade crossing. Above, the steam locomotive water tank is at right, and beyond it is the express house of the Railway Express Agency. Moving farther east and to the north side of the tracks, Weber photographed the express house with the water plug at the west end of the building. The station building is in the distance. The baggage house and PD Tower are in the far distance at left.

Weber photographed PD Tower from Ocean Avenue on May 19, 1943. The tower, constructed of wood, opened on May 29, 1912. The block operator in the tower controlled the Patchogue track switches and the Ocean Avenue grade crossing gates. In the above photograph, looking south, the tower is on the right beyond the storefront. The building to the left, on the south side of the tracks, is the old Brookhaven Town Hall. Below is a photograph facing north showing the tower at left. A widow's walk is visible on the roof of the building on the other side of the tracks. Straight down Ocean Avenue in the distance is the Swezey and Newins Department Store.

A light layer of snow has dusted PD Tower in this January 1972 photograph taken by David Keller. On days like this, the wooden outdoor stairs became treacherous because of the ice that coated them. The second window from the left has a bracket on the side. These brackets were where train order boards were originally placed to indicate to train crews that they had orders.

This April 6, 1963, photograph by William Lichtenstern shows a pair of Budd Rail Diesel Cars (RDCs) on the north siding at Patchogue. These cars were used in Scoot service, running back and forth between Patchogue and Babylon. The baggage house and PD Tower are at right, and the South Ocean Avenue grade crossing is in the distance at center. (Courtesy of David Keller.)

On a snowy day in December 1970, David Keller photographed RS3 No. 1559 pulling the westbound Scoot from the north siding over the crossover switches and onto the main track at PD Tower. The block operator has his stick in the air, and the engineer is about to grab his orders for the shuttle run to Babylon.

In this 1971 photograph that David Keller took from an upper window of PD Tower, block operator H. Edward Sorensen is hooping up the train's orders to engineer George Becker. This eastbound Train No. 4 was headed for Montauk with an Alco C420 locomotive at the head end and a baggage car behind. Although the locomotive has a large "M" (the symbol for the Metropolitan Transportation Authority since 1968) below the cab window, the baggage car still sported an earlier Dashing Dan emblem, which the MTA would soon entirely eliminate.

49

Renowned agent/operator James V. Osborne took this photograph of block operator Al Bunker at the levers inside PD Tower in March 1930. These levers were mechanically linked to the track switches and signals via connecting rods. (Courtesy of David Keller.)

Win S. Boerckel took this undated photograph from the upper stairway platform of PD Tower. An eastbound passenger train, led by a steam locomotive, is approaching the tower, where the engineer will pick up his train orders. The building at left is the baggage house. (Courtesy of Win A. Boerckel.)

In January 1970, David Keller took this picture of the grade crossing watchman standing in front of the Bay Avenue shanty east of Patchogue Station. To the right of the shanty is the old wooden bin from which the watchman would retrieve coal to feed the potbelly stove inside the structure. The watchman's means of communication was a telephone housed in the "T" box on the pole behind the shanty.

The Greater Patchogue Historical Society is fortunate to have a preserved LIRR grade crossing shanty in its collection. It is on display behind the historic Swan River Schoolhouse in East Patchogue. (Courtesy of the Greater Patchogue Historical Society.)

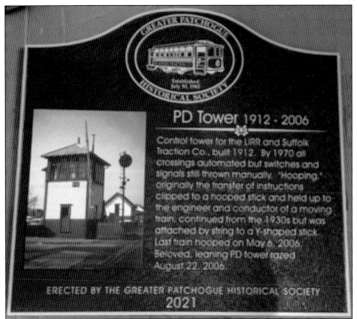

The location of the former PD Tower will be commemorated this year with the placement of this plaque, which will be mounted at the Ocean Avenue grade crossing where the tower was once located. (Photograph by the Greater Patchogue Historical Society.)

Of the 11 tugboats that the LIRR used to own for its car float operation, one built in 1907 had the distinction of being named *Patchogue*. It is shown here crossing New York Harbor in October 1944 with the New York City skyline in the background. This tugboat was scrapped in 1959, and LIRR maritime operations were suspended on October 31, 1963.

Four

HAGERMAN TO EASTPORT

Hagerman Station, 2.7 miles east of Patchogue, was opened in 1890 as a flag stop. A small, box-type wooden station was built, as shown in this c. 1925 photograph taken by agent/operator James V. Osborne. In 1929, this station stop was removed from the LIRR timetable.

Bellport Station opened in the summer of 1882 as a wood-frame building with canopies on each side. This c. 1925 photograph of the building was taken by agent/operator James V. Osborne. A kerosene platform lamp is in the foreground at right. The agency closed in January 1959, and the building was razed in May 1964; it was replaced by a metal shelter shed. (Courtesy of David Keller.)

This September 20, 1958, photograph of Bellport Station faces southwest and shows the rather large trackside agent's bay. The depot was razed in May 1964. This station stop was targeted to be closed in the late 1990s, when the LIRR was constructing high-level platforms at all stations. Through the efforts of community leader Miles Boone, the station was saved, and a short, high-level platform was installed. (Courtesy of David Keller.)

Brookhaven was added to the LIRR timetable in 1884. A wood-frame building with canopies on each side was erected, as shown in this c. 1925 photograph by James V. Osborne. The agency closed in 1932, and in 1944, the building underwent a remodeling that included the removal of the canopies and the Victorian gingerbread. (Courtesy of David Keller.)

This October 15, 1952, nighttime picture by Richard Wetterau shows the Brookhaven Station building as it appeared after the 1944 renovation (without canopies). The station stop was discontinued on October 6, 1958. The building was moved off-site and became a private residence.

In 1882, a station stop named Forge was established four miles east of Brookhaven. In 1893, its name was changed to Mastic. A small wooden building was erected, as shown in this c. 1900 photograph facing northeast. The uniformed man on the platform is most likely the station agent. Note the absence of canopies at the sides of the building. An old-style block signal is in front of the agent's bay. (Courtesy of David Keller.)

In the 1920s, the Mastic Station building underwent a renovation that included adding small canopies on each end of the building and extending the roofline over the agent's bay. This September 2, 1948, photograph by Fred J. Weber shows the renovated structure at right. This picture was taken from Mastic Road looking northeast.

These photographs were taken by Fred J. Weber on September 2, 1948, at the Mastic Road grade crossing. In the above image looking north, is it apparent that there were no watchmen or gates at this crossing. A portion of the station canopy is at right. In the below image looking east, freight cars are at right on the passing siding. The switch in the foreground controls the track leading to the freight house. The round device next to the switch is the switch indicator, which shows which way a switch is aligned. The only way to confirm the alignment of a switch is to observe the gap of the switch points.

This nighttime photograph of Mastic Station was taken by Richard Wetterau on October 17, 1952. This building was razed in August 1960, and the station stop was moved 7,000 feet west; a small brick building was erected and is currently still on-site. The name of the station was changed to Mastic Shirley, but even the MTA website sometimes refers to it as Mastic-Shirley.

Fred J. Weber took this picture of the east end freight/express house at Mastic on June 16, 1949. Mile marker 63 is at right. The remoteness of this area is illustrated by this photograph. The freight house was mounted on a raised platform to facilitate the transfer of freight and express to and from box and express cars.

In 1881, LIRR started service out of Centre Moriches. A wooden station building was constructed with canopies on each end and an extended roof on the plaza side. As shown on this real-photo postcard postmarked August 22, 1911, the roof had finials on each end and a rooftree running the length of the roof. The destination sign reads "Centre Moriches." An express house is visible in the distance. A Hawkins taxi is parked at the depot.

This postcard, which was created later than the 1911 image at the top of this page with the automobile in view, shows that horse carriages were still the main street transportation at that time. The roof finials and rooftree have been removed. Note the open windows of the railroad cars at the platform. The sign on the carriage in the foreground reads "Centre Moriches Livery."

This photograph of the Center Moriches Station building was taken by Richard Wetterau on October 17, 1952. Note that the destination sign reads "Center Moriches." The spelling of "Centre" was changed to "Center" in February 1943 at the request of the local chamber of commerce. A baggage wagon is visible underneath the west canopy.

This photograph facing southwest was taken at the Center Moriches Station building in October 1958. The building was razed in May 1964 and replaced with a metal shelter shed. In 1985, the metal shed was replaced with a small wooden shed.

On January 20, 1998, the author, facing west, took the above photograph of the Center Moriches Station. The Railroad Avenue grade crossing is in the distance. This picture was taken during the final days of the station. On March 16, 1998, the station was permanently closed (see below). This was one of 10 stations closed that day due to low passenger usage. The other stations that were closed on the Montauk Branch were Quogue (see pages 79–80) and Southampton College (see page 86). These closings led to cost savings for the LIRR because expensive, high-level platforms would not have to be constructed at these locations.

Center Moriches

To Our Customers:
Station To Close March 16

Effective Monday, March 16, the Center Moriches station will close.

Trains will no longer operate to or from this station.

Transportation Alternatives:

Customers may wish to travel east to the Speonk station or west to the Mastic-Shirley station.

Please consult November 17, 1997 timetables for current train service to or from all stations. Remember to consult the new timetables which will become effective March 16.

 Long Island Rail Road

LIRR 24-Hour Travel Information Center	
• New York City and Jamaica	(718) 217-LIRR
• Nassau	(516) 822-LIRR
• Suffolk	(516) 231-LIRR

These two postcards show the 1891 East Moriches station building. This structure was built using $1,500 in contributions by local residents. The above trackside view looks southeast and shows a steam locomotive approaching the station. Note that the building is on an embankment and has a wide stairway leading down to the platform. There was a pointed tower over the agent's bay. LIRR historian Ron Ziel said that this tower gave the station the appearance of an Eastern Orthodox church. The below view faces northeast and shows the plaza side of the building. Finials and a rooftree adorned the roof. The freight house is in the distance. This beautiful station building burned to the ground in 1936.

LIRR Claims Department photographer Fred J. Weber took this picture of the Pine Street grade crossing of East Moriches on April 12, 1946. The switch leads to the track siding for the Red Comb Mills plant, with its tall storage silo. The grade crossing shanty is at left, as well as the diamond-shaped warning sign. The view in the distance illustrates the remoteness of this area.

After the original East Moriches station building was lost to fire in 1936, the LIRR erected a smaller brick structure, as shown in this June 20, 1955, photograph looking southeast. On October 6, 1958, this station stop was discontinued, and the building became a private residence on-site. (Courtesy of David Keller.)

Block operator James V. Osborne climbed the semaphore signal in 1923 and captured this westward view at PT cabin west of Eastport Station. Looking toward the junction of the Manorville Branch, the Montauk Branch curves in from the left in front of PT cabin. Across the tracks is the section house. In the foreground at left and right are the two passing sidings. (Courtesy of David Keller.)

This is a close-up picture of PT cabin also photographed by James V. Osborne. At junction points where only a few switches were involved, the LIRR would set up a standard design cabin to provide shelter for the block operator. The Pennsylvania Railroad referred to these structures as Frame Signal Buildings. The chimney in the center of the roof provided a vent for the smoke from the fire in the potbelly stove. This view looks east toward the block signals.

In 1870, LIRR president Oliver Charlick built a branch from the main line in Manorville south to Eastport (called Moriches at the time) and farther east to Sag Harbor. This was intended to stave off the South Side Rail Road attempting to build eastward from Patchogue. The 1870 station building is pictured in this 1907 postcard view facing west. Note the jigsaw scrollwork under the edges of the eaves and the wooden passenger cars at the platform. Also note the block signal and the open-air express house in the distance.

The Eastport Station building is visible to the southwest in this 1923 photograph by James V. Osborne. The fancy jigsaw scrollwork is gone, but there is still a kerosene lantern on the platform to provide lighting at night. This stop was taken off the timetable on October 6, 1958, and the building was moved off-site for private use.

We have a gage house on this July 8/07.
stream — Walter.

A short distance east of Eastport Station, trains travel across a small stone bridge over the Seatuck Creek. This 1907 postcard shows a nice reflection of the bridge in the creek and has interesting handwriting at the bottom indicating that there was a "gage house" on the stream. A water gage would send an early warning if the water was rising to flood level. The writer, Walter, put the date on the card as July 8, 1907. A man and a dog are on the bridge.

This postcard could be said to represent an iconic view of early-20th-century railroading on Long Island, as a steam locomotive is hauling a passenger train over the Seatuck Creek Bridge in Eastport. This idyllic image was also used on note cards.

Five

SPEONK AND WESTHAMPTON

A station building was erected at Speonk in February 1870 along what was then the Sag Harbor Branch. In 1879, George Brainerd took this photograph looking southeast toward the building and freight/express house. On June 22, 1901, the building was struck by lightning and burned to the ground.

A new station building opened at Speonk in December 1901. As shown in this 1907 image, it was a wooden structure with a wraparound roof overhang rather than canopies on each side, as at many other stations. This building was identical in design to the one at the Blue Point station, which opened in the same year (see pages 35–36). According to LIRR historian Ron Ziel, the Speonk and Blue Point buildings were delightful aberrations from the usual design at LIRR stations.

East of Babylon, many trains terminate at Patchogue or Speonk rather than the end-of-the-line terminus at Montauk. At Speonk, there is a layup yard on the north side of the track. There is also a wye for turning trains. In the days of steam locomotives, there was a water tank to replenish the tenders. This John Krause photograph, which looks east and was taken in the late 1950s, shows C-liner No. 2008 at Speonk with the water tank at left.

On January 13, 1949, Fred J. Weber photographed a passenger train at Speonk, as shown in these two pictures. The above image faces west and shows a good view of the scalloped roof support brackets of the building. The chimney was for the potbelly stove in the waiting room. The below image looks east from the Phillips Avenue grade crossing and shows the building. The freight house is in the distance, and two crew members are on the platform getting ready for the train's departure. The grounds around the building were unpaved. The kerosene lantern has been replaced by bare-bulb lights on concrete posts.

It was not too often that LIRR Claims Department photographer Fred J. Weber went inside a station building for his job, but on the day that he took the pictures shown on the previous page, he also photographed the waiting room. The above photograph shows the potbelly stove and, oddly, a sink to the left of the stove. A portion of the ticket office is at far left. The below photograph shows the trackside waiting room door and the ticket office to the right. This cage-like enclosure allowed heat from the waiting room stove to enter the ticket office. Preserved ticket offices like this one may be viewed at the railroad museums in Wantagh and Lindenhurst.

On September 16, 1973, the last wooden water tank from the LIRR's steam locomotive era was demolished at Speonk and photographed by engineer of structural maintenance H.G. Campbell Jr. Sadly, not one of these relics of the past was preserved. (Courtesy of Win A. Boerckel.)

The Speonk agency closed in 1958, and the building fell into a period of disuse. The LIRR—and later, the MTA—rented the building for use as a breakfast and lunch facility. This July 6, 2013, photograph shows the building when it was known as the Track Side Café. It is now vacant once again. Fortunately, the exterior of the Speonk building has been preserved in its original form, unlike its sister building at Blue Point.

Similar to the Speonk Station facilities shown on page 67, Westhampton received both station and freight/express buildings in 1870. In 1879, George Brainerd photographed Westhampton on the same day he photographed Speonk. Here, a freight scale is visible on the raised platform at the west end of the station building. The remoteness of the area is evident.

In 1905, the original Westhampton Station building was demolished, and a new two-story brick structure was erected. This 1918 valuation photograph looks north and shows the architectural beauty of the building with two double-window dormers on the second-floor level. The upstairs served as the living quarters for the agent and their family. A large plaza is in front of the building.

Long Island R. R. Station, Westhampton Beach, L. I.

These two images show the Westhampton Station building from the trackside facing southwest. The 1912 postcard view above shows the building prior to the installation of the passing siding, which was installed a few years later to the right. The substantial number of second-floor dormers is evident. Below is a painting by local artist Elizabeth Duerschmidt, who specializes in capturing nostalgic scenes from Westhampton's past. The single row of four columns supporting the east-end canopy stand out in this image. Most station canopies are supported by two rows of columns. The artistic beauty of the Westhampton Station building is exemplified in this painting.

The Railroad Station, Westhampton, L. I.

Westhampton Station was popular in the summer months, when vacationers flocked to Long Island's beach resort towns. People would get off the express trains, such as the Cannonball, and head for the town of Westhampton Beach and its sandy beaches. In the early 1900s, horse-drawn carriages met the trains at the station, as shown in this postcard view. The freight house is at far right near Depot Road.

This 1915 Thomas R. Bayles photograph, taken at Westhampton Station facing west, shows mailbags being loaded onto the Railway Post Office (RPO) section of a passenger combine car for a westbound return trip from Montauk. The last day of RPO service on the LIRR was June 18, 1965, when train No. 32 carried mail to Montauk. (Courtesy of David Keller.)

On August 24, 1995, an explosive and massive wildfire swept through the pine barrens region of Long Island, which included the Westhampton Station area. On that evening, the author (who was the branch line manager at that time) drove east to Speonk Station to supervise the busing program, since train service was suspended east of Speonk. The author took this photograph showing the smoke caused by the wildfire farther east. This image shows the height of the smoke as it appeared over the roof of the station building. The author was quickly instructed to go to Westhampton Station.

Long Island Rail Road

Date December 21, 1995

DEC 2 7 1995

To D. Morrison, Branch Line Manager

From John J. O'Connor - Chief of Police

Re Employee Commendation AWC #95-45

Please accept the enclosed Certificate of Appreciation for your assistance to this Command on August 24, 1995.

I am advised by members of my staff that you assisted members of this Department in gaining access to the ticket office at Westhampton Station during the Sunrise Fire. You also helped them remove the ticket cabinet from the office, when the fire was dangerously near that location.

You are to be commended for your courage and commitment to the protection of company property. Had it not been for your help, the company may have lost a substantial amount of ticket stock.

Again, please accept my personal thanks for all assistance rendered and a job well done.

When the author arrived at Westhampton Station on August 24, 1995, the night of the wildfire, there was a small area of fire on the roof, and railroad ties in front of the building were on fire. Pungent smoke filled the air, and fire was working through the trees as it approached the station from the north. As firefighters pushed back against the blaze, with the help of LIRR police, the author entered the building, went into the ticket office, and retrieved the ticket case, reserve ticket stock, and other valuable items. As the author was taking the items away, he called upper management to let them know that the station building would probably not be there in the morning. The LIRR chief of police at the time, John J. O'Connor, presented a certificate of appreciation to the author along with this commendation letter.

The above image looks west on August 25, 1995, the morning after the fire, and shows the new, high-level passenger platform at Westhampton Station in the early stages of construction. The station building is visible at the left side of the far end of the platform. To the right are the burned-out trees on the north side of the tracks. Below is another photograph looking west taken at the platform outside the station building. An eastbound Montauk train, pulled by GP38-2 locomotive No. 251, is entering the station. To the right are the burned trees. At this point, the track department had already placed ties on the ground to prepare for the replacement of the fire-damaged ties. The fire also jumped the tracks and damaged buildings and vehicles on the south side of the station.

In another morning-after photograph from August 25, 1995, a westbound passenger train from Montauk enters the station area pulled by MP15ac locomotive No. 171. Fire-blackened trees are visible at left. At the time of this writing, more than 25 years after the wildfire, the area has turned green again.

After the fire on August 24, 1995, a Westhampton Beach Fire Department truck was parked at the station as a precaution in case of flare-ups. The station building is visible beyond the fire truck. Affectionately referring to themselves as the "Sons of the Beach," the valiant firefighters saved the historic Westhampton Station building from being destroyed.

Six

QUOGUE TO WATER MILL

LIRR service started at Quogue in 1870 with only a rickety wooden platform on posts. In 1875, a wooden station building and freight house were erected, as shown in this 1876 photograph taken by George Brainerd. This building was replaced in 1882 with another farther west that lasted until 1905, but there are no known photographs of that second station building.

In 1905, a rather substantial two-story brick building was erected at Quogue. This postcard image faces northwest and illustrates the architectural beauty of the building with the three second-floor dormers and the overhanging roof above the first floor. The canopies on each end were supported by central columns in a manner similar to those at the Westhampton Station building. The steam locomotive water tank is in the distance at left.

In this 1912 photograph, a passenger train is at the station and cars are parked at the platform, with the Quogue Station building in the distance. The 1905 building was demolished in April 1964 and replaced with a metal shelter shed. The station was taken off the LIRR timetable on March 16, 1998—one of 10 LIRR stations abandoned that day.

The first station building at Good Ground opened in 1871 but burned down two years later. This photograph shows the second building, which opened on January 10, 1874, with a combination of horse carriages and early automobiles at the station. The plaza was simply dirt. This building was moved farther east in 1913 and used as a freight house.

A two-story brick Colonial-style structure with canopies on each end replaced the wooden building at Good Ground. This June 6, 1918, valuation photograph shows the track side of the building with the tall signal semaphore mast in front of the agent's bay. The name of the station was changed to Hampton Bays in 1922 to attract visitors to the beach. The building was razed in 1964 and replaced with a metal shelter shed.

A short distance east of Hampton Bays Station, there is a fenced-in grave site south of the tracks. This is the grave of celebrated Shinnecock minister Rev. Paul Cuffee, who was buried here in 1912. LIRR train engineers still give a couple of toots on the horn to pay tribute to this legendary Native American preacher.

Between Hampton Bays and Shinnecock Hills, the railroad passes over a bridge that crosses the Shinnecock Canal. In 1898, after an earlier bridge proved to be unsatisfactory, the LIRR built a 210-foot-long iron bridge across the canal. In this 1915 photograph looking north taken by T.R. Bayles, the bridge is seen from the Montauk Highway. (Courtesy of David Keller.)

In 1931, a new and much stronger steel bridge was built across the Shinnecock Canal to allow heavier locomotives to access Montauk. This photograph looks west. To the left of the track, just before the bridge, a low cinder platform known as Canoe Place served as a stop for the Fishermen's Special trains that the LIRR ran between 1935 and 1953. (Courtesy of David Keller.)

The Canoe Place stop got its name because this was where members of the Shinnecock tribe would put their canoes into the water to cross to the other side. Brad Phillips has this Canoe Place ticket and a Fishermen's Special brochure in his collection. The fishermen could store their fishing gear and coolers in the baggage car; many of them went all the way to Montauk to fish.

This August 7, 1960, photograph shows westbound train No. 4007 being pulled by engine No. 2002 coming off the Shinnecock Canal bridge. This bridge opened on June 13, 1931, and allowed the LIRR to run heavy K4s steam locomotives across the canal. It was nicknamed the "K4 bridge" as a result. This bridge weighs 800 tons, whereas the older bridge weighed 215 tons. The 1931 bridge is still in use today.

In 1907, a seasonal flag stop named Suffolk Downs was opened between the Canoe Place and Shinnecock Hills stations. The stop was discontinued in 1927. This photograph shows the small station building in the winter of 1927 with its windows and doors boarded. When the stop was discontinued, agent James V. Osborne purchased the building and had it moved to become his personal summer residence.

In 1887, LIRR president Austin Corbin established a station stop at Shinnecock Hills and had quite an elaborate building erected to serve as a sales office for his real estate development company. The ticket agency closed in 1931, but the building doubled as a post office. This August 16, 1963, photograph taken by Norman Kohl shows a westbound passenger train going past the station building where the mailbag would be captured on the fly.

At Shinnecock Hills, postal employee Janet Jordan was hanging a mailbag on June 17, 1965, for the afternoon westbound pickup by the RPO car, which would snag the bag while the train was traveling at 30 miles per hour. The next day, RPO service on the LIRR ended after 130 years. There are no RPO cars currently preserved on Long Island.

At the same time Suffolk Downs Station opened in 1907, a seasonal flag stop named Golf Grounds was created near the 1891 Shinnecock Hills golf course. This station was discontinued in 1939, and the building was moved a year later to become a private residence. Four US Open championships have been held at this golf course—in 1896, 1986, 2004, and 2018.

On May 20, 1976, a new station stop opened at the site of the former Golf Grounds flag stop. The station was named Southampton College and was created to serve students at the nearby college. This photograph shows the ceremonial opening of the station with LIRR president Walter L. Schlager Jr. (holding a shovel and nearest to the camera). This station also served those attending the 1986 US Open. The station closed on March 16, 1998.

The station at Southampton opened in February 1871 with a wooden station building and freight house on the south side of the tracks. This c. 1880 photograph—taken by George Brainerd and looking west—shows both buildings, which had finials at the edge of the roofs. These buildings were demolished in 1902 when a new building was erected with lengthy platforms and express houses constructed on each end.

Pictured here in an October 25, 1917, valuation photograph looking northeast is the 1902 Southampton Station building. The exterior was stucco with embedded oyster shells enhanced by brick bordering around the windows and doorways. Note the lengthy east-end canopy with the express house at the far end. The architect was Bradford Lee Gilbert, who is discussed in more detail on page 34.

The beauty of the embedded oyster shells and the decorative brickwork at Southampton Station are evident in this July 25, 1986, photograph of agent Charlie Muller standing in the trackside doorway. Muller was the agent at the station for several decades prior to his retirement in 1988. Under Muller's care, the ticket office interior and waiting room were supplied with all sorts of antiques. After Muller left, the "museum" was cared for by agent Larry Shea.

In the words of the late LIRR historian Ron Ziel, "Southampton—inside and out—is indisputably the most handsome train station on Long Island, and one of the finest anywhere." The cover of the July 1950 issue of the *Long Island Railroader* employee magazine illustrates the beauty of the waiting room with its long oval bench in the center and fireplace along the east wall.

Water Mill first appeared on the timetable in 1875. Unfortunately, there are no known photographs of the original depot building. A brick building with canopies at each end was constructed in 1903 and is pictured in this October 25, 1917, valuation photograph. The station stop was discontinued in 1956, but the building survived. It has been beautifully rebuilt and is now the central portion of an office/condominium complex.

Here is a beautiful sight of an early steam locomotive–hauled passenger train with smoke billowing as it crosses over a bridge with an old wooden mail car in the lead. LIRR historian Ron Ziel wrote "Water Mill" on the back of this photograph, but that location is questionable. This c. 1906 photograph does present a classic view of early railroading on the east end of Long Island.

LIRR historian Ron Ziel owned a house at 265 Mill Pond Lane in Water Mill for a number of decades. A second-floor columnated open-air porch offered an excellent view of Montauk Branch trains. Sometime in the late 1990s, for unknown reasons, Ziel moved the house to Southampton. Ziel passed away on December 15, 2016. Above is a photograph of the house with an eastbound passenger train going past it. The engineers frequently gave a few toots of the horn when passing. Below, the house is shown crossing over the tracks on its way to Southampton. Fresh fill underneath the truck indicates that the roadway had to be raised to prevent the trailer from bottoming out.

Seven

BRIDGEHAMPTON TO AMAGANSETT

The LIRR opened a station at Bridgehampton as part of the railroad's expansion from Manorville to Sag Harbor in 1870. A depot building opened in June 1870 but burned to the ground in July 1884. Shortly thereafter, another building was erected; it is pictured on this 1910 postcard. A horse-drawn carriage is waiting at the wooden platform as an eastbound steam locomotive approaches for a station stop.

This 1896 photograph shows a crew posing next to their train at Bridgehampton Station. This was the shuttle that ran back and forth to Greenport by way of Manorville Junction. A portion of the station building is visible at left; note the chimney for the potbelly stove and the sawtooth decoration at the canopy's edge.

Train No. 4008, pulled by locomotive No. 2402, is shown approaching Bridgehampton Station on August 16, 1959. The depot building, which was in its final days when this picture was taken, is at left. The decorative wooden features that beautified the structure were gone, and the canopy had a noticeable sag.

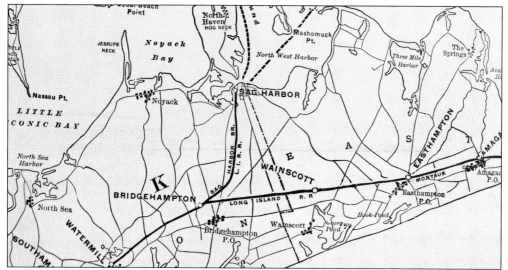

This c. 1930 LIRR map shows the Sag Harbor Branch as it diverted from the Montauk Branch at Bridgehampton. The stations at Water Mill and Wainscott, which are shown on this map, no longer exist. Sag Harbor was the east end, south shore terminal for the LIRR until the railroad was extended to Montauk in 1895.

When the Sag Harbor Branch was created in 1870, there were no station stops between Bridgehampton and Sag Harbor. A stop was established as Noyack Road in 1908, and a small shelter shed built in 1922 is shown in this 1923 James V. Osborne photograph. This shed was demolished on May 3, 1939, when the Sag Harbor Branch was abandoned.

The LIRR reached Sag Harbor in 1870, and a station building was erected the following year. It was positioned perpendicular to the end of the track, as shown in this c. 1873 photograph by George Brainerd. Many old terminal station buildings were constructed parallel to the end of the track. This building burned down in 1873.

A board-and-batten building replaced the Sag Harbor station structure that was lost to fire; it was later moved to the side of the track, as shown in this 1903 photograph. The 0-4-6T steam locomotive No. 327 is at the platform with a man standing next to it. This building lasted until 1910, when it was replaced by a larger brick structure.

The 1920s were still horse-and-wagon days, as is evident in this June 23, 1924, valuation photograph of the Sag Harbor express stable. The wagon was possibly stored behind the large door on the right side of the building. The ramp outside the door on the left side was most likely for horses.

In May 1901, the LIRR constructed a spur track to the "Long Wharf" for the purpose of running coal-hopper cars to service steamboats. The pier was owned by the Montauk Steamboat Company, which was an affiliate of the LIRR. Steamboats traveled across Long Island Sound to Connecticut. This 1907 postcard shows a hopper car next to a ferry at the end of the spur.

The R. R. Station,
Sag Harbor, L. I.

Pictured on these postcards is the two-story Dutch Colonial gambrel roof–style Sag Harbor Station building erected in 1910. There was a porte cochere extending from the building on the plaza side. This construction was funded by Sag Harbor resident Olivia Slocum Sage, the wife of railroad tycoon Russell Sage. The above image shows the station building when it was new. The old station building is at right, and the express house is at left. In the below postcard, the old station building is gone, and to the left, a horse and wagon are at the express house. When the Sag Harbor Branch was abandoned in 1939, this building was used as an office for a local fuel company until it was demolished in February 1966.

Railroad Station, Sag Harbor, L. I.

At the west end of the Sag Harbor Station was an express house, which was closed on one end and open on the other with a canopy extending over it. This November 8, 1917, photograph looks northeast and shows the express house on a raised platform with a passenger train in the background at left.

After the Sag Harbor Branch was abandoned in 1939, the Sag Harbor express house was privately purchased and moved to a new location. The open end was enclosed, and the building now houses the Sag Harbor Garden Center on Spring Street. Jean Held took this photograph in 2012 in front of the garden center building. Pictured here are, from left to right, Diane and Phil Bucking (proprietors of the Sag Harbor Garden Center) and Elaine Lewis.

In 1927, the LIRR obtained two self-propelled gas cars, known as doodlebugs, from the Pennsylvania Railroad. The doodlebugs were designed to carry mail, express, and passengers on short runs, and the LIRR used them mainly east of Port Jefferson on the Wading River Branch and the Sag Harbor Branch. These photographs were taken in April 1939, one month before the line was abandoned. Above, gas car No. 1134 is at Sag Harbor Station. The below photograph was taken at Sag Harbor on the same day and shows three men posing with the car—the conductor and engineer and a man in a business suit who was most likely a railroad official.

Gas car No. 1134 is pictured at Sag Harbor with the station building behind it on July 5, 1935. The cooling radiator is visible above the coupler. These gas cars were the subject of many passenger complaints, mainly because of the loud noise they made when running and the gasoline smell. They were the forerunners of the Budd Rail Diesel Cars (RDCs).

A short time after the Sag Harbor Branch was abandoned, the Pennsylvania Railroad sold the gas cars. Car No. 1134 was sold to the Atlantic & Western Railroad of Sanford, North Carolina. This photograph shows the car in an advanced state of decay at Sanford. The fate of the car is not known, but it was probably scrapped.

The 1898 depot building at Wainscott was replaced in 1915 with a more substantial structure, which is shown in this 1923 photograph looking west. A steam locomotive hauling a passenger train is at right, passing the freight/express house as it approached the station. There was no siding track at this station. The Wainscott station stop was abandoned in 1938, and the building was moved off-site to become a private residence.

In 1925, James V. Osborne photographed Wainscott Station looking east. Note that the building had two chimneys due to the fact that there was a potbelly stove in each of the two waiting rooms. This building had two segregated waiting rooms because the summer residents did not want to mix with the migrant farm workers. This was the only LIRR station building to have segregated waiting rooms.

When the LIRR was extended from Bridgehampton to Montauk in 1895, three station buildings were erected that were identical in design: Farmingdale on the main line and East Hampton and Amagansett on the Montauk Branch. These stations were one-story brick structures with canopies on each side. At the ends of each canopy were wide-sweeping wooden arches. Pointed dormers, sans windows, were on the front and rear roofs. This 1907 postcard faces northeast and offers a good view of the East Hampton Station.

Looking west down the wooden platform, this 1912 photograph shows a passenger train at East Hampton Station with steam locomotive No. 4 (a 4-4-2 type). The station building was on raised ground and required a long stairway with four steps to go down to the platform. On the left, a wooden ramp for baggage extends from the platform. Horse carriages are in the station plaza.

East Hampton was a busy station during the summer months, with many people going to the south-shore towns of Long Island to enjoy the beaches. The above photograph offers a good view of the stairway that ran the length of the station and the freight house at the east end. Below, quite a crowd is getting off the train, and one man preferred going up the grass embankment instead of the crowded stairway. A bare-bulb gooseneck lamp provided lighting at night.

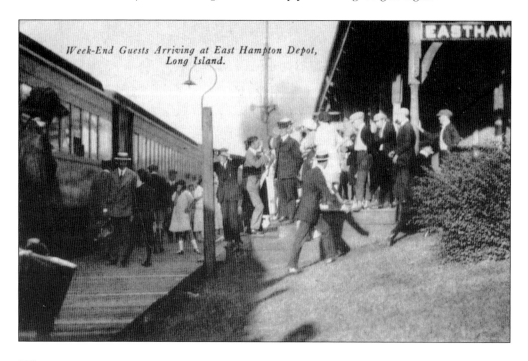

Week-End Guests Arriving at East Hampton Depot, Long Island.

The first grade crossing east of East Hampton Station is Newtown Lane, which is pictured in this photograph taken on July 15, 1948. Here, eastbound Train No. 10 (a Saturday-only train) is pulling out of the station with Pennsylvania Railroad–leased steam locomotive No. 230 at the head end. The freight house is at left.

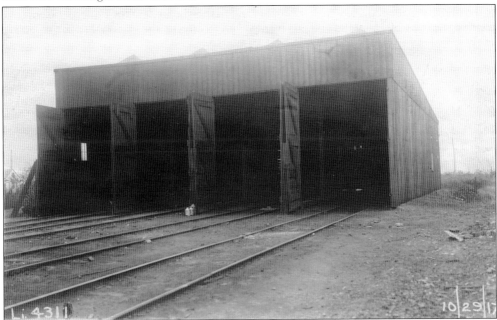

The LIRR preferred to keep its steam locomotives out of inclement weather by laying them up inside engine houses that were spread out over the system. One such facility was a four-stall engine house at Amagansett, shown in this October 29, 1917, valuation photograph. This structure was demolished in 1928, when the Pennsylvania Railroad decided to consolidate engine service facilities at the Morris Park Shops in Jamaica.

The 1895 Amagansett Station building is pictured in this 1909 photograph. The similarities to East Hampton Station may be easily recognized. This picture is rather unusual, because all of the people are identified. They are, from left to right, Howard Eichhorn (Western Union messenger), Ira Baker (station agent), Louis Schmidt (telegrapher), Frank Tibbets (young boy), Craven Vaugh, and George Eichhorn (locomotive engineer).

In 1910, the original Amagansett Station building was destroyed by fire, and a two-story Dutch Colonial structure was erected in its place. In this c. 1912 photograph, station agent Ira Baker (at far left with his young daughter standing in front of him) poses in front of the building with a group of unidentified people. A comprehensive history of Baker written by LIRR historian David Keller appears on the website trainsarefun.com.

This is the Amagansett Station building as it looked in 1911. This is the building where Nazi spies, having arrived on the beach by submarine, purchased train tickets for New York City on June 13, 1942, to engage in acts of sabotage. Fortunately, they were arrested after arriving in the city—and before they were able to do any damage. This building was demolished on August 31, 1964, and replaced with a shelter shed.

This 1949 postcard offers an excellent view of the Amagansett Station area looking east, with the freight house visible on the left. It might seem strange, but that freight house survives to this day, even though most LIRR freight houses have been demolished. Currently, freight on the LIRR is handled by the New York & Atlantic Railway.

View showing Public School, Amagansett, L. I.

Sometimes, images of historic LIRR railroad stations appear in surprising places. While searching for Amagansett postcards, the author was fortunate to come across these two. The above postcard was listed under the heading "Amagansett, LI, NY public school" but offers a great view of the Amagansett Station building in the distance. Similarly, the below postcard was advertised as "Amagansett Long Island NY World War Memorial." Again, another nice view of the train station is in the background. Both of these images illustrate the remoteness of the area around the station. As an aside, the schoolhouse was torn down in 1937; the war memorial is most likely still in place.

World War Memorial
Amagansett, Long Island, N. Y.

Eight

MONTAUK

A 8171 R. R. Station, Montauk, L I.

When LIRR service began to Montauk on December 17, 1895, a single-story wooden structure served as the train station. Due to the fact that this was the last station on the line, there was no need for an agent's bay window nor a semaphore signal mast. In this postcard view, children are on the wooden platform, and a uniformed man stands in the doorway.

Austin Corbin—who was president of the LIRR from December 31, 1880, until his untimely death on June 4, 1896—was responsible for extending the railroad to the eastern terminal of Montauk. He had visions of developing a deepwater port at Fort Pond Bay in Montauk, but those plans were scrapped after his death. This bust of Corbin is at the Putnam Museum and Science Center in Davenport, Iowa.

For a brief time, from 1903 to 1927, there was a flag stop known as Napeague Beach between Amagansett and Montauk. A small shed and short raised platform existed at that stop, as shown in this c. 1924 photograph looking east taken by James V. Osborne.

In 1911, the original Montauk Station building was greatly expanded to the rear, and a second floor was added to offer living quarters for the agent and their family. The first floor also contained a post office, express office, and a town hall with a jail. This structure was razed in 1927, when a new building was constructed perpendicular to the end of the track.

Looking west from the bluffs, this c. 1920 photograph presents a panoramic view of Fort Pond Bay at right and the Montauk facility at left. The two-story station building is to the right of the smoke-billowing locomotive, and the freight house is to the left. A steamship is visible in the bay.

In July 1898, the US War Department chose Camp Wikoff at Montauk to be its port of debarkation for troops returning from the Spanish-American War. Troops getting off boats in Brooklyn and Long Island City were transported by LIRR trains to Montauk for a period of quarantine before going home. This photograph features Col. Theodore Roosevelt addressing the troops who gained fame as the Rough Riders.

The most famous LIRR train is arguably the all–first class, all–parlor car train the Cannonball, which ran from Long Island City to Montauk. In 1899, Hal B. Fullerton photographed the first run of the Cannonball at the Montauk fishing platform. Most of the men on the walkway leading to the pier are wearing straw hats. In later years, the parlor car trains were known as "straw hat specials."

A train is arriving at Montauk Station in 1932 with a Pennsylvania Railroad K4s locomotive at the head end, followed by an RPO car and heavyweight parlor cars. This building, which opened on June 1, 1927, along with a new yard, was perpendicular to the tracks. In 1942, the US Navy took over the property and used this building as an office facility. The building still exists as a private residence. (Courtesy of David Keller.)

After the US Navy took over the 1927 Montauk Station building, the government constructed a new building a short distance south. It was almost identical in design to the former building, but it faced parallel to the track. In this early-1950s photograph taken by John Krause, C-liner locomotive No. 2403 is backing out from the station and headed for the yard and the wye.

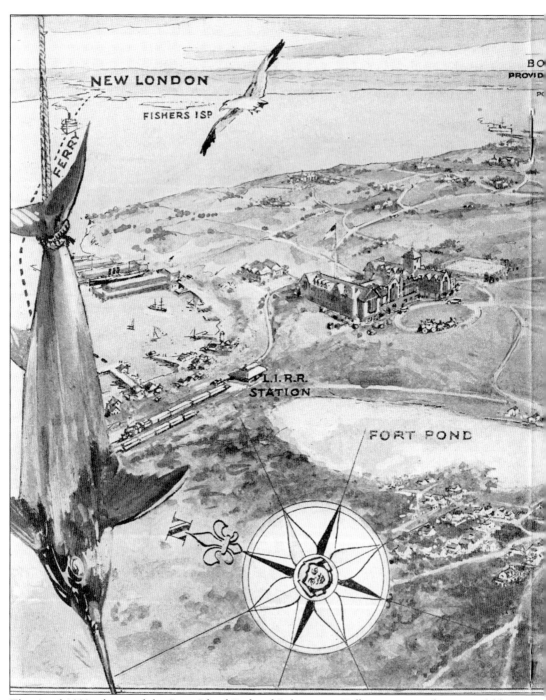

The April 1929 edition of the *Long Island Railroad Information Bulletin* contained a centerfold spread drawing of Montauk, facing northeast. The railroad station is to the left of Fort Pond. The Montauk Manor hotel is a short distance northeast of the station on a hill; this hotel appears in many photographs of trains in the layup yard. The Long Island Sound is to the left, and the

Atlantic Ocean is to the right. The Montauk Point Lighthouse, which was constructed in 1796, appears in the upper right corner. This lighthouse is one of the most famous landmarks on Long Island, and an image of it appears on many LIRR publications, including timetables, brochures, and advertising posters.

1926 SCHEDULE
of the
"SUNRISE SPECIAL"
Pullman Cars Only—No Coaches

To THE HAMPTONS *and* MONTAUK

READ DOWN p.m.	STATIONS	READ UP a.m.
3.19	New York (Penna. Station)...	10.12
....	Westhampton	8.27
5.14	Quogue	8.21
5.34	Southampton	8.04
5.39	Watermill	....
5.46	Bridgehampton	7.52
5.58	Sag Harbor................	7.14
d5.52	Wainscott	....
5.59	Easthampton	7.41
6.10	Amagansett	7.34
6.25	MONTAUK	7.15

From May 19th to June 28th and from September 10th to about October 15th, this train will be operated eastbound on Fridays and westbound on Mondays.

Between June 28th and September 10th this train will run DAILY, except Sundays.

Westbound train will not be operated from Montauk except from June 28th to September 10th, inclusive.

See regular time-table schedules for other daily and special Saturday, Sunday and Holiday service to The Hamptons, Montauk, Sag Harbor and intermediate stations.

MONTAUK POINT—AT THE END OF THE SUNRISE TRAILS

LONG ISLAND RAILROAD COMPANY.

To demonstrate its solidarity with the Sunrise Trail theme, the LIRR went so far as to change the name of its Cannonball, the Friday afternoon express train from Penn Station to Montauk. In the summer of 1922, the Cannonball was renamed the Sunrise Special. This 1926 advertising poster promotes the "Pullman Cars Only" train. Note the image of the Montauk Point Lighthouse.

The LIRR Sunrise Trail led to the Montauk Point Lighthouse, which appeared on the cover of the November 1950 issue of the *Long Island Railroader*, an employee publication. These employee publications appeared in the form of magazines—rather than newsletters—from 1950 to 1955. The covers always had color title boxes at the top. Except for this issue and December issues, all of the *Long Island Railroader* covers featured railroad-themed photographs.

The Montauk freight house is pictured in the center of this November 29, 1952, photograph, with the station building at left and the Montauk Manor hotel on the bluff at right. In the early 1960s, the freight house was moved to Industrial Road, and it still stands today as a private residence.

The 1942 Montauk Station building is shown on this undated postcard with the Montauk Manor hotel in the background. The ticket agency ended full-time service on January 21, 1972, and it was open during summers only until it was permanently closed. In 1998, the MTA leased the building to the Montauk Artists Association, which currently has a gallery and offices there. Train tickets can be purchased at nearby vending machines.

This photograph of Montauk Station was taken on April 10, 1996. The 1942 station building is at right, and the yard tracks are in the foreground. The second structure from the left (in the distant background, partially blocked by trees) is the 1927 station building, which is still in its original location and now serves as a private residence.

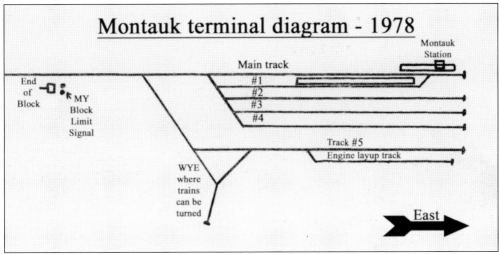

Montauk terminal diagram - 1978

Montauk Station

Main track

End of Block

MY Block Limit Signal

Main track
#1
#2
#3
#4

Track #5
Engine layup track

WYE where trains can be turned

East ➤

The Montauk terminal yard tracks are shown in this 1978 diagram, which is not to scale. The main track goes to the station building, where it dead-ends. The yard tracks are south of the station. Track 3 is the longest track in the yard, and was where the Cannonball was stored for the weekend. Track 5 comes off the wye, where entire trains can be turned.

On March 25, 1946, LIRR Claims Department photographer Fred J. Weber took this picture, looking northeast from Industrial Road, of a leased Pennsylvania Railroad K4s locomotive, with a baggage car behind, negotiating the west leg of the Montauk wye. The water tank is to the left, and in the distance at right is the Montauk Manor hotel.

LIRR G5s steam locomotive No. 35 is shown in the Montauk Yard in this 1946 photograph looking southwest. The water tank is visible above the locomotive. This locomotive is currently being restored for static display at the Oyster Bay Railroad Museum.

This is a typical scene in the Montauk yard with trains laid up over the weekend. Two GP38-2 diesel locomotives and numerous 2900-series passenger cars await return westbound trips on Sunday evening. This July 1998 view looks east with the Montauk Manor hotel in the background. The station building is in the distance at far left.

On May 5, 1963, Brad Phillips took this photograph in the Montauk yard, facing east. RS3 diesel locomotive No. 1556, at left, is currently part of the equipment collection of the Railroad Museum of Long Island in Riverhead. Next to it is C-Liner No. 2404 with a string of parlor cars behind it. The Montauk Manor hotel is partly visible behind the C-Liner.

In the early 1950s, John Krause photographed a westbound train from the bluffs overlooking Fort Pond Bay with the Montauk Manor hotel in the background. That photograph appears on page 63 of his book, *Long Island Rail Road*. John Scala commissioned artist Howard Fogg to paint the scene based on Krause's photograph. The painting shows C-Liner No 2402 at the head of the westbound train of parlor cars.

Effective June 5, 1995

The Hamptons and Montauk
Summer Timetable

- **Montauk**
- **Amagansett**
- **East Hampton**
- **Bridgehampton**
- **Southampton**

In 1995, the LIRR decided to celebrate the 100th anniversary of the start of its train service to Montauk. An anniversary logo was designed and placed onto the summer timetable for the Hamptons and Montauk. As shown here, the June 5, 1995, timetable had the logo on the cover (in color). At the bottom of the logo is a design that represented the tracks going toward the sunrise. At the top is a drawing of the Montauk Point Lighthouse. Through the years, the LIRR has used the lighthouse to promote train service to the east end of Long Island. On October 7, 1995, an anniversary ceremony was held at Montauk Station. The event was attended by MTA chairman E. Virgil Conway, LIRR president Thomas F. Prendergast, and Long Island Sunrise Trail Chapter of the National Railway Historical Society president Benjamin Young.

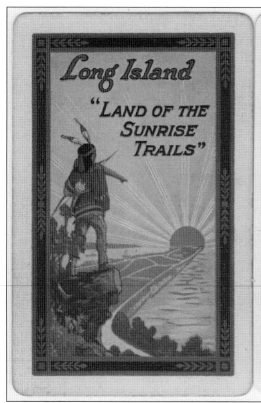

During the Montauk 100th anniversary year in 1995, the LIRR produced a souvenir deck of playing cards. Carol Mills had a deck of 1921 LIRR playing cards, which she suggested could be used as the design for the new cards. Because the LIRR was concerned that the Native American image would not be appropriate, a drawing of a GP38-2 locomotive with a Cannonball logo on the head end was used. These are images of the 1921 (at left) and 1995 playing cards.

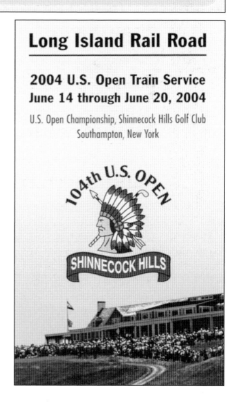

An image of a Native American was used by the LIRR on timetables for trains servicing the US Open at Shinnecock Hills. The LIRR used the image because it was the logo used by the US Golf Association. Although it is shown here in black and white, the original timetables featured the image in color.

In late 1967, Ron Ziel and George Foster (coauthors of *Steel Rails to the Sunrise*) planned to create a tourist railroad utilizing the former right-of-way of the Sag Harbor Branch. They wanted to operate their line under the name Sag Harbor and Scuttle Hole Railroad. The name Scuttle Hole referred to a village in the Water Mill area near Ziel's home. Ziel and Foster arranged a fundraising train trip from Jamaica to Montauk using the leased Black River & Western Railroad 2-8-0 steam locomotive No. 60 with a consist of coaches. The leased engine cost $2,500 to rent plus $1,500 for insurance. These two photographs were taken at Montauk during the November 26, 1967, trip.

Here are two more photographs of steam locomotive No. 60 at Montauk on November 26, 1967. Above, the locomotive is at the end of the main track with the Montauk Station building at left. Below is a view of the observation car that was at the rear end of the train during the run. The trip went fairly well, with just a few minor glitches, until the westbound trip back to Jamaica. The train was in the Massapequa Park area when the steam locomotive died. It took several hours before it could be towed to Jamaica by a diesel locomotive. The road-foreman-of-engines was in the cab for the entire trip and said that he had been instructed by upper management to "give the people a good time, but don't let that locomotive come back to Jamaica under steam."

On September 19, 1998, at Montauk Station, the LIRR joined the community in celebrating the period when Colonel Roosevelt and his Rough Riders were quarantined at Camp Wikoff after their return from the Spanish-American War. The station plaza was in deplorable condition, with huge potholes. For two weeks before the event, the branch line manager (the author) had been promised by the engineering department that the plaza would be repaired. The day before the event, the author was told that the work would not be done. Upon hearing that, the author telephoned the vice president to remind him that the MTA board chairman, the LIRR president, and dozens of members of the Tampa Rough Riders—with horses—would be at the station. The author was instructed to not go home until the repair work had started. Around 6:00 p.m. that evening, a dump truck the size of a tractor-trailer arrived from the Hudson Valley with a load of bluestone, and the work began. This photograph was taken as the bluestone was being unloaded. The next day, the plaza looked fine, and the event commenced without a flaw.

A train fitted with a centennial celebration drumhead took passengers and centennial celebrants to Montauk on September 19, 1998. At the head end of the train was a Metro North Railroad FL-9 locomotive followed by double-decker cars. The train arrived at the new platform, where passengers walked down a ramp and east toward the station area. This photograph shows the locomotive with the "crossed swords" Rough Riders logo on the drumhead.

Pictured here getting off the train and heading toward the Montauk station on September 19, 1998, are MTA chairman E. Virgil Conway (wearing a top hat) and his wife, Elaine (holding a parasol). They were portraying Pres. William McKinley and his wife, Ida. In the background at left, the FL-9 locomotive is next to the platform canopy.

Nearly 100 members of the Tampa Rough Riders attended the centennial celebration, with many of them on horseback. Officially named First US Volunteer Calvary Regiment—Rough Riders Inc., the group was founded in 1978 for the purpose of "creating and perpetuating a living memorial to the unique accomplishments of President Theodore Roosevelt and the Rough Riders." Above, the Rough Riders parade around the station plaza. Below, they position their horses for the start of the ceremony. At left is a large tent that was set up next to the station building. The Montauk Manor hotel is at right.

This photograph in the archives of LIRR historian and author David Keller is an appropriate image to end this book. In the words of Keller:

Montauk station is the end of the LIRR's Montauk branch and nothing says end of the line like this eastward view of PRR-leased E6s No. 1600 sharing old engine layup track number one with a couple of freight cars. The locomotive is steaming in preparation of a westbound passenger run. In the background are the bluffs barren of trees, with bare white patches of sand showing through the scrub growth. Atop the bluffs, overlooking all like a king viewing his kingdom, is the famed Montauk Manor, a windswept landmark for many years. It's summer, 1939 and, as the Montauk branch comes to an end, so, too, many other things are soon to end with a world war about to begin.

DISCOVER THOUSANDS OF LOCAL HISTORY BOOKS FEATURING MILLIONS OF VINTAGE IMAGES

Arcadia Publishing, the leading local history publisher in the United States, is committed to making history accessible and meaningful through publishing books that celebrate and preserve the heritage of America's people and places.

Find more books like this at
www.arcadiapublishing.com

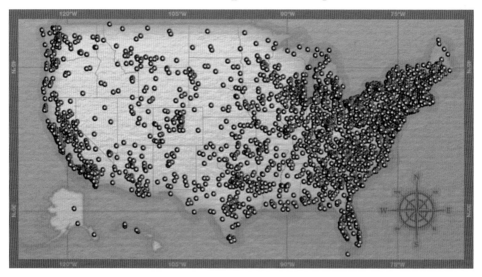

Search for your hometown history, your old stomping grounds, and even your favorite sports team.

Consistent with our mission to preserve history on a local level, this book was printed in South Carolina on American-made paper and manufactured entirely in the United States. Products carrying the accredited Forest Stewardship Council (FSC) label are printed on 100 percent FSC-certified paper.

MADE IN THE USA